USING PERISCOPE FOR BUSINESS

How to Engage Your Audience with Live Streaming

RYAN BATTLES

Title: Using Periscope for Business
Subtitle: How to Engage Your Audience with Live Streaming

ISBN-13: 978-1516926220
ISBN-10: 1516926226

To Heather,

For all of your support and watching the kids while I write from coffee shops and hotel lobbies.

— Ryan

CONTENTS

YOUR TWO FREE GIFTS

Before we dive into the wonderful world of Periscope, and how it can benefit your business, I wanted to let you know about a special gift that I have for you to thank you for picking up this book.

It can be found at https://ryanbattles.com/periscope-bonus

ESSENTIAL RESOURCE GUIDE

One of the chapters goes into gear that you can use for a quality scope broadcast. I refrained from linking to any specific products because I wanted this book to be a little more timeless and not link to products that have been updated or discontinued.

As a result, I've created a PDF download of recommended equipment for creating high-quality scopes, something that I can keep up-to-date, and is going to have the most recent links to where you can find these products.

NOTABLE ACCOUNTS TO FOLLOW

While the world is waking up to Periscope and more and more accounts are created, there are a few notable people that have been rocking it with Periscope, and frequently hold broadcasts to give additional tips and ideas on how to leverage Periscope for its maximum business potential.

This book provides a solid foundation for getting started with Periscope, even diving into some advanced tips, but the education doesn't have to stop there. Download this list of notable accounts of people who are using Periscope to grow their businesses.

To download this list of notable accounts to follow, as well as the resource guide, head over to:

https://ryanbattles.com/periscope-bonus

WHAT OTHERS ARE SAYING ABOUT PERISCOPE

When I first heard about Periscope, I dismissed it as a "new hot fad" that would come and go and shouldn't receive much of my attention. However, in the coming weeks I began to notice a lot more buzz around it, and thought that perhaps there might be more to this live streaming app. Many of the entrepreneurs, marketers, and successful businesses that I follow on social media have been jumping on the bandwagon, and seem to have a pretty bright outlook on the growth potential of live streaming, specifically with Periscope. I'm convinced that this is more than a passing fad or a shiny new app that will lose it's luster, and I don't seem to be alone:

"For me, Periscope is about intimacy and simplicity. No editing. No webinar slides. No countdown timer. No commercials. And if done correctly and consistently I believe Periscope will become the go-to platform for personal brand builders who wish to deepen their relationship with their audience."

—**Chris Ducker**, Founder and CEO of Virtual Staff Finder[1]

"Live streaming is something I think is going to be huge, so when I heard Twitter had acquired a new company that does just that, I was intrigued. Peer to peer live interactions are clearly here, and on the rise. Snapchat dabbled in it with their new chat function that launched about a year ago...because Periscope will be owned by Twitter, the seamless transition between the apps is inevitable, and we will probably see embedded images, and maybe even the ability to watch live streams in feed."

—**Gary Vaynerchuk**, Author of Crush It[2]

"On a personal level, I think the implications of live-stream content are absolutely mind-boggling."

—**Marcus Sheridan**, Founder of The Sales Lion[3]

---

[1] http://www.chrisducker.com/periscope-to-build-your-personal-brand/
[2] http://www.callowaygreen.co.uk/c4p_log/log-8055/
[3] http://thesaleslion.com/live-stream-economy-brands

"You can give exclusive previews of products, how-to tutorials, a quick tour of your facilities, or show off your services. And, of course, you will have the potential to respond in real time to feedback from viewers."
— **Troy Evans**, PPC Analyst at Distilled[4]

"I believe this is a GAME CHANGER for businesses who are looking to grow their business."
— **Derek Halpern**, Entrepreneur and Speaker[5]

"I really am starting to see the bigger picture here with the value of live streaming. It's a fantastic way to deliver additional value to your audience and bring your tribe even closer to you."
— **Chris Marr**, Founder of the Content Marketing Academy [6]

---

[4] https://moz.com/blog/twitch-phenomenon-live-streaming
[5] https://socialtriggers.com/how-to-use-periscope
[6] http://www.callowaygreen.co.uk/periscope-for-business

"To me, this is valuable primarily for its immediacy. I get unmediated, real-time input from customers, stakeholders and people interested in social media. I've had suggestions for future updates to my own product (including a Periscope integration), as well as feedback on what we need to be doing better and questions about features in the pipeline. Yes, some commentary is off-topic. But most of it is relevant, even eye-opening."

—**Ryan Holmes**, CEO of Hootsuite[7]

"In case you haven't noticed, I'm a little bit excited about Periscope. Think webinars but for busy people, via your phone and with loads more interaction – 'one with many' instead of 'one to many' I heard someone describe it as."

—**Dan Norris**, Author of Content Machine[8]

"Periscope is a natural acquisition for Twitter allowing it to offer an additional value-added experience which extends Twitter as a media platform and not just a sharing platform."

—**Brian Solis**, Author of The End of Business as Usual[9]

---

[7] https://www.linkedin.com/pulse/how-you-can-use-hot-new-apps-meerkat-periscope-business-ryan-holmes

[8] http://dannorris.me/periscope-tips/

[9] http://www.briansolis.com/2015/03/meerkat-ephemeral-state-livestreaming-tv/

ABOUT THIS BOOK

Periscope is one of those tools that you can figure out pretty easily just by downloading it and trying it out. In fact, you can easily grow your business using Periscope without reading this book, simply by diving in and live streaming on a regular basis.

So why should you read a book on Periscope for business?

I wrote this book because when I started using Periscope, I knew that I loved what I saw, but didn't quite understand the potential use cases. There were many questions that I asked myself when I first became acquainted with the Periscope:

- How were people using Periscope other than to film themselves eating cereal?

- Are businesses using this? How so?

- Why does that guy use a selfie-stick when he broadcasts?

- Do I need equipment to run a broadcast?

- What's the deal with those hearts?

- Why is everybody using emoji characters in their titles?

- When I start a broadcast, do I just start talking or are there some tips on how to start a broadcast off successfully.

- How do I encourage people to share these broadcasts and grow my following?

- How can I be a better participant when watching other broadcasts, will this help my own following?

- What are the security and privacy implications of live streaming? How do I mitigate those?

- What happens to my broadcast after I finish? Is there a way to go beyond the 24-hour replay window Periscope provides?

- How is this different from YouTube?

- What should I say in my bio to maximize impact?

- How do I deal with obnoxious comments while broadcasting?

- How can I convert this audience into customers for my business?

- How do I develop a game-plan for where Periscope fits into my marketing strategy?

- Where is Periscope heading?

Why is the Nasdaq live streaming their closing bell? Are they the only business using this thing? Who's watching?

I wrote down as many questions as I could think of when getting started with Periscope. Then, I was determined to figure it all out by watching hours of broadcasts, going through previous broadcasts to see how they've evolved. I scoured social media accounts outside of Periscope to see how people are sharing their broadcasts with existing networks, and read over 100 review articles on Periscope, and how others are using it for business. Of course, I also started broadcasting with Periscope, anything from describing my processes and office setup, to interviewing colleagues, to answering questions while grilling dinner.

This book is the culmination of many hours of research and information gathering, so it could all exist in one quick-read volume. My goal is to not only get you over the small learning curve to understanding the ins and outs of periscope, but more importantly, to help you brainstorm ways to leverage it to:

- Grow your business

- Increase your audience

- Improve your bottom line

It is my heartfelt belief that Periscope can do this for you, as it already has for many others that I've interviewed for this book.

INTRODUCTION: THE POWER OF LIVE STREAMING

My very first experience using the Internet was 20 years ago, before every home had a network connection. I was in the school library during study hall, and was one of the few kids who knew how to use the computers in the back of the room. I'm not sure the librarians even knew what I was doing back there every day, since the most common use for the machines was looking up books in the digital card catalogue.

I had discovered that after navigating to the card catalogue, selecting the public library link to expand my search, then scrolling down to the bottom of the page, there was a lonely text link that simply stated: The World Wide Web.

Now, these computers were so old that they didn't even have graphics capability, they were text-only. That didn't stop me, being able to access a world outside of my school, while I was in study hall, was all I needed. I eventually found out how to join a chat room, where other students from around the world had figured out how to get on the web, and by constantly refreshing the page and leaving messages, we could hold conversations in real time.

I made friends with students in Singapore, Brasil, and London. There were people there from California to New York, and many places in-between. Before this time the only way you could communicate with people across the world was waiting weeks for traditional mail to reach them, or pay a small fortune to call long-distance.

The world has changed dramatically since then, but only in the methods that we use to communicate in real time. The fascination is still there, whether you are a student in study hall or a grandparent connecting with loved ones far away. What was once a futuristic video phone from The Jetsons has now become the tiny smartphone in nearly every pocket.

THIS BOOK IS ABOUT MORE THAN PERISCOPE

While the technology over the past 20 years has gone beyond what just about anybody could have imagined, I can't even fathom what life will be like 20 years from now. What is nice to remember is that it is simply the tools that are changing, but the principles of digital interaction remain constant. The rules of business and marketing still apply the same today as they did thousands of years ago.

As business owners, our goal is not to learn how to overhaul the fundamentals of business, marketing, communication, networking, growth, etc. Rather, our goal should be to take stock of the current tools available to us at this day and age, and leverage them for maximum impact.

Periscope is one of the newer tools on the scene, owned by Twitter, a company that has proven its staying power as a social tool, and is likely not going away anytime soon. It offers the ability to live-stream anything that your phone's camera sees, in real-time, with no second takes. Viewers can interact by sending "hearts", and chatting directly into the room. It's raw, it's unpolished, and people are drawn to it.

This book aims to explain the fundamentals of using Periscope, what it is, how to leverage it, and strategies for growing your business using this exciting new tool. The goal is not to simply become a "Periscope Master", but to have a plan and purpose for using Periscope to grow your business.

TRANSPARENCY AND COMMUNITY BUILDING

With literally thousands of other social media networks out

there, what makes a live streaming app like Periscope worth investigating? The answer in four words: Transparency and Community Building.

First of all, transparency.

Because Periscope broadcasts live, unedited footage from the host's camera, there is an unparalleled sense of authenticity to it. This footage has not been ported into a video editing suite for special effects or removal of mistakes. It has not been censored or edited by anybody before it reaches your eyes. What has been said cannot be taken back, and what you see is happening in real time.

There are no 5 second delays for editing like a halftime show at the super-bowl. Of course, this can also make Periscope an ideal lurking ground for some of the less-admirable types of content of the Internet. Thankfully for those of us hoping to use Periscope for business, the company has a policy against certain types of content and will ban users for violating this. Because anybody who views a scope can report it, this is a fairly effective policy that keeps the majority of content on Periscope quite innocent.

While there are tradeoffs to this type of transparency, and let's face it, not being able to edit the broadcast is a little nerve-wrecking for some people, the level of authenticity portrayed through a scope is rare in today's world. People trust what they see on a scope, and this leads to a greater bond to the broadcaster when viewing.

Periscope is also a great community-building tool.

I have been following the content of Dan Norris[1] for some time now. He writes great articles on entrepreneurship and marketing, while he shares specific details about his wins and losses along the way. His transparency has always been something that attracts me to his content, and this is why I follow his blog, read his books, and interact with him on Twitter.

Dan is also a huge fan of Periscope. He is one of the earliest adopters, using Periscope to reach out to his community on a regular basis. In the past 2 days I have joined scopes with Dan as he shares tips from a beachfront rental on the gold coast of Australia, as well as a silly moment shared laughing with friends in the living room during another scope. I'm getting to participate in a small slice of his world, deepening the connection I feel to his content.

According to a recent Forbes article, "People ultimately choose to do business with people they like."[2] Granted, there are a wide variety of factors that play into why we may or may not like someone, but what intrigues me about this statement is the use of this phrase: "choose to do business with people." A personal connection is much more likely to garner a business relationship vs. dealing with a faceless company.

Leveraging Periscope to put some personality into your business, whether it is specifically business-related or the occasional laughing with friends, it helps us to connect with each other, and

[1]   http://dannorris.me/
[2]   http://www.forbes.com/sites/amyanderson/2013/06/28/people-do-business-with-people-they-like/, retrieved August 17, 2015

build communities together. Periscope allows you to follow others and receive notifications when they are broadcasting. You can also share a broadcast with your followers on Periscope, which expands the network effect for those who are producing high-quality content.

EXAMPLES OF COMPANIES LEVERAGING PERISCOPE

At the time this book was written, Periscope had only been out a few months. However, there is no shortage of businesses jumping in and using it to expand their platform. Already companies have discovered unique ways to engage with their audience, build brand awareness and loyalty, and educate their target audience.

In the next few pages, we're going to take a look into exactly how some of these companies have been using Periscope to grow their businesses.

CNN

As the Royal Baby Charlotte arrived in May 2015, CNN correspondent Max Foster was live-streaming footage from inside the media cordon at the Lindo Wing hospital. He also streamed live reports from Buckingham Palace, as well as various other spots around London, even while he was walking down the street!

While the rest of the world had to wait to watch the news coverage once an hour during the 60 second update on CNN's broadcast channel, Periscope viewers were given a real-time account of the events unfolding, and were able to ask questions directly to Max and share comments with the rest of the participants.

This move quickly established Max as a news source to follow in regards to the Royal Family. Many who participated in his broadcasts no doubt experienced a greater connection to him, and are now more likely to tune into CNN when looking for news coverage, or at least Max's account on Periscope.

RED BULL

The news casting potential of Periscope is an obvious one, but what about a company that sells a product? That's exactly the type of question the Red Bull team had to discuss in order to embark on their Periscope strategy.

Red Bull has live-streamed various events, such as Miami Music Week, the Redbull Baylines competition in San Francisco, and even parties streaming from their infamous Red Bull Guest House. For a company that is trying to connect with a generation of young, excited, active individuals, they seem to be hitting the nail on the head with their Periscope strategy.

DORITOS

Combining a variety of social media tools owned by the same company (Twitter, Periscope, and Vine), Doritos was one of the first brands to use Periscope as a platform for a contest.

Chosen randomly from the Periscope viewing audience, individuals would win a prize based off of a spinning wheel of nachos corn chips. The winners were also announced on the video-sharing site Vine.

You may wonder how spinning a wheel of chips helps Doritos improve its bottom line. The secret is in brand awareness, and community building. No doubt they grew their subscribers on all three of those social networks — who wants to miss out on the next contest?

DKNY

Soon after the Periscope app hit the iOS app store, DKNY shared behind-the-scenes tours of their DKNY fashion closet, a first-hand look into the world of a major clothing company.

It wasn't the highest quality stream out there, and it may have given a few viewers motion sickness due to the hand-holding of the phone used to shoot the video footage, but they made waves by giving exclusive access to Periscope viewers, and are commonly referred to anytime using Periscope for Business is mentioned.

Note, we will discuss how to shoot higher quality video in a later chapter, so you can avoid the shakiness that plagued the DKNY broadcast.

SPOTIFY

With competition from Rdio and Apple Music, Spotify is a music streaming service that has continued to find ways to differentiate itself in a fierce marketplace. Shortly after the launch of Periscope, the lead singer of the Irish indie folk band Villagers, Connor O'Brien, recorded an impromptu jam session and streamed it live.

What makes an early adoption of Periscope so important for a company like Spotify is that their main focus is a mobile-based music service. Their target audience is people who use their smartphones for entertainment, so providing a live jam session to bring in hundreds of viewers was clearly a step in the right direction.

GENERAL ELECTRIC

I'll have to admit, even I was shocked to see General Electric — a company founded two centuries ago — on the Periscope train.

Companies like Red Bull and Doritos are expected to dabble in new technologies to reach the youngest generations, but a blue-chip company like GE?

Perhaps they have been around for so long because they know how to stay relevant. At first GE used Periscope to go behind-the-scenes on StarTalk Radio with astrophysicist Neil deGrasse Tyson and Bill Nye the Science Guy. This alone would have been an impressive use of a new platform for such a large company, but they've since gone on to do something even more spectacular: #DRONEWEEK.

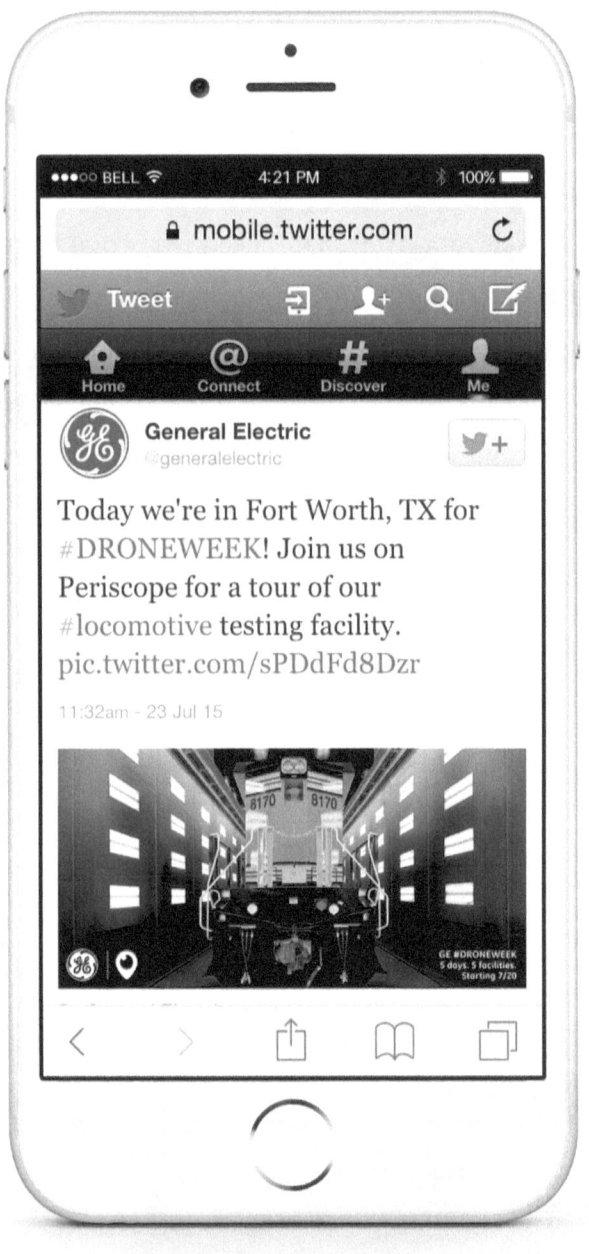

General Electric announcing #Droneweek

That's right, an event that is named with a hashtag, built from the start to be a viral social phenomenon, GE spent 5 days touring 5 facilities with drone cameras, sharing sights never before made public. Viewers were given access to the facilities where jet engines, locomotives, and wind turbines are manufactured and tested for durability.

It is hard to form an emotional attachment to a company so impersonal as GE. Even the name, "General Electric" does very little to evoke a personality of any type. However, latching on to technologies such as Periscope, they are educating people on how their products affect our everyday lives, potentially even inspiring new engineers for the future.

ADIDAS

The first major sports company to embrace Periscope was Adidas. When Columbian soccer superstar James Rodríguez signed a deal with the company from their Herzogenaurach, Germany headquarters, they streamed the 20 second event to Periscope, and brought in viewers by announcing it on their Twitter account.

It was a small broadcast, but a powerful one. It shows how Periscope can break down the barriers between audience and company in order to deepen an emotional connection. Because Periscope broadcasts are expected to be quick and raw, there are many use cases for putting out a new broadcast, sometimes you just need to try a few things and see what sticks.

STRATEGIC USES FOR PERISCOPE

Perhaps when reading a few of the examples of how companies are using Periscope in the previous chapter, you came up with some ideas of your own. As more and more businesses latch on to Periscope, new ideas and use cases will become clear. Already a few types of scopes have become popular for business use:

BEHIND THE SCENES

Like DKNY did with their fashion closet, a behind the scenes look at the way a business is run makes for good content.

One of my favorite shows growing up was Reading Rainbow. In each episode, in addition to reading a book, the host would take the viewers behind the scenes to learn about how products are made. It was fascinating as a child, and it is fascinating to me now. People love to see behind the scenes, there is a sense of mystery about each door that is labeled "Employees Only."

In your own business, what is behind-the-scenes may not seem that interesting, but you'll have to remember that it isn't interesting to you perhaps because you see it every day. For people in a different field, even the smallest details might be interesting.

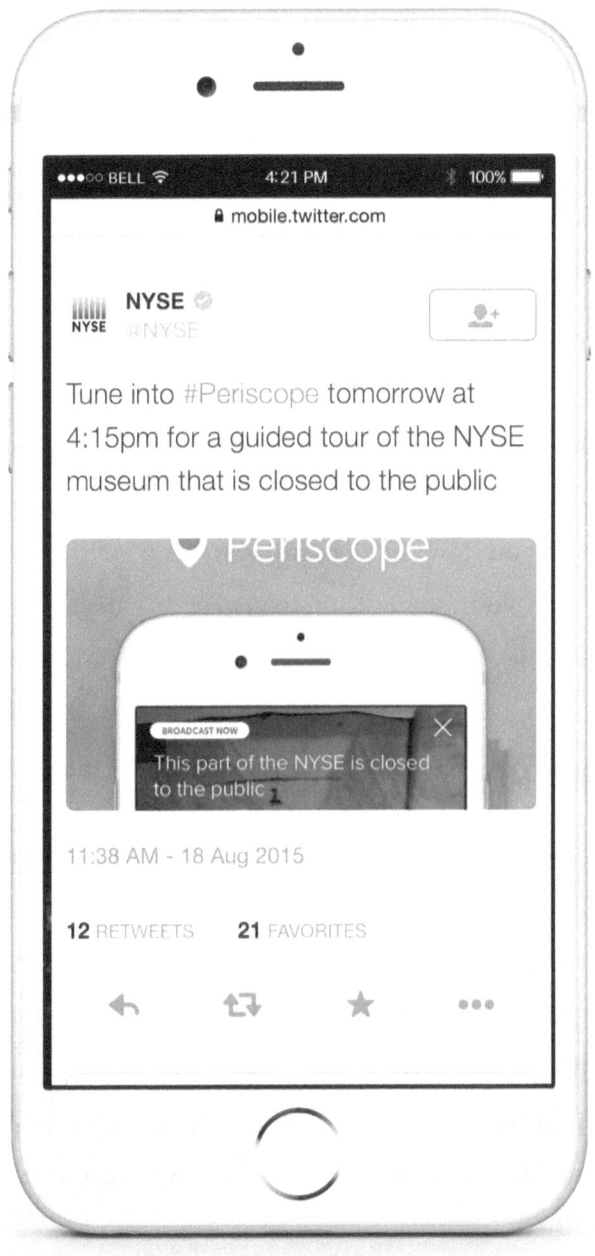

Use Periscope to go behind the scenes

NEW PRODUCT FEATURES

Whether your product is physical or digital, Periscope is a great place to show off a new product feature, discussing the story behind it, the work needed to make it happen, and answer any questions that your audience may have.

Of course, random passers-by on Periscope might not be interested in your product, or its new feature, but because each scope can be shared easily on Twitter, those who are already following your company might be very interested in watching your broadcast. Even if you don't have many viewers from the get-go, you can still promote your scope to viewers for the next 24 hours. Sometimes the replay viewers easily outnumber the live ones.

ANNOUNCEMENTS

When sharing an announcement, building up anticipation is key. For example, if you have news to share that your audience would be interested in knowing about, instead of announcing it in a traditional press release, why not announce on Twitter and Facebook that you will have a live scope with the announcement at a specific time tomorrow? You can simply tell them to visit your Twitter profile at that time for the link, or follow you on Periscope to get notified.

Of course, you can still use a traditional press release and any other tactics you use to spread new announcements for your business, but the advantage of live streaming is that people are able to connect with you and experience the announcement immediately as it happens. People love feeling like they are a part of something exclusive, like being in at ground zero when something exciting is announced.

LIVE TESTIMONIALS

Because Periscope broadcasts are raw and real, a customer testimonial carries a lot of weight. In fact, it can be pretty scary as a business owner because you have no idea what the person is going to say! However, a Periscope testimonial carries a lot of credibility in the eyes of the viewers for this reason. It is the equivalent of a Yelp or Amazon review that is out of the control of the product owner, and that can be an advantage.

Recently I stumbled across a yoga instructor who was chatting with her clients after a class. She was asking them what they thought of the class, what was the hardest part, and how they feel afterwards. Even though they were still sweaty and somewhat out of breath, they took questions from Periscope and spoke candidly about the class.

Of course, if this is a Yoga studio 500 miles away I will probably never become a customer, but the instructor could definitely use Periscope broadcasts like this to share on Facebook with those who are in her community. In fact, she could develop a following around the world with enough interesting content and begin selling instructional videos digitally.

LIVE EVENTS

If there is a controversial aspect of Periscope right now it is the unlicensed sharing of events. Whether a sports game or concert, the fact that anyone with a phone can stream the content to the world in real-time is raising some legal department eyebrows. However, if you are the one behind the event, such as Adidas' contract signing with James Rodríguez, then stream away.

Some forward-thinking musicians are already streaming footage of their concerts from the stage. I spent an evening recently doing housework to a live stream of a concert by one of my favorite bands. Did that live-stream make me less likely to purchase an album from the band or attend one of their concerts? No way! Again, any time a bond is strengthened between a business and its audience, good things are happening for that business.

Public speaker and marketer David Meerman Scott spoke recently at a Tony Robbins Business Mastery Conference, and broadcast his talk via Periscope. While the conference itself typically has a large audience, David reported that nearly as many people watched his scope than were in attendance to the live event.[1]

If you are going through the trouble of putting an event together, why not simply setup a phone, tablet or iPod Touch to broadcast the event on Periscope as well?

INSTRUCTIONAL VIDEOS

Many companies have already realized that an informative blog can help establish them as thought leaders within their industry. For some, YouTube has become a place where they share instructional videos to grow their audience. In many cases, this same content can be broadcast on Periscope as well in order to take advantage of the real-time feedback that the audience provides.

I have already stumbled across cosmetic companies who are broadcasting tips for applying makeup over Periscope. Content marketers and authors are giving quick tips on their subject matter, with well over 1,000 viewers per broadcast. Leveraging Periscope for how-to videos is another way to re-purpose content, so you can get the most mileage out of the same amount of research.

Note: in a later chapter I am going to go into how you can save your videos beyond the 24-hour archive in Periscope to create a long-lasting library of content.

---

[1] http://www.webinknow.com/newsjacking-my-talk-via-periscope-at-tony-robbins-business-mastery, retrieved on August 17, 2015

FLASH SALES

If anything lends itself well to the time-limited nature of live streaming, it is a 24 hour flash sale. This is a sort of twist on the announcement scope, but basically you could use Periscope to announce a coupon code good only for the next 24 hours, while this scope is live. Ask you audience to share the link to the scope with their friends, and create a sense of urgency.

You will likely grow your following for this type of scope because people will want to be notified when this happens again.

GIVEAWAYS

Like Doritos did with their tortilla wheel, come up with a fun way to give away prizes to people who are watching the broadcast. If you are giving away multiple items, make sure to take time in-between giveaways to allow attendees to invite their friends in using the built-in sharing tools. Again, this is a great way to grow your audience as people will want to know when the next giveaway is.

As far as getting information from the winners, each of their accounts is tied to a Twitter profile, so you can simply ask them to direct message you their contact information via Twitter to get the goods to them appropriately.

RESEARCH

Because viewers of a scope can send messages and hearts as feedback, Periscope can be a great place to bounce ideas off of a crowd in a short amount of time. For example, when writing this book I was designing the cover myself, and wanted to know if it was eye-catching or needed work. I quickly setup a Periscope broadcast and focused my camera on an image of the book cover and solicited feedback. You'll be surprised at other's willingness to share their thoughts simply because you asked.

Q&A

In the opposite vein of crowd-oriented research, instead of asking a question to your audience, open up an opportunity for them to ask you questions. One of the most popular types of forum threads across the Internet in recent times is the AMA, or "Ask Me Anything". Typically, the title goes: "I'm the X at Y company, ask me anything."

On the popular social news website, Reddit, a few of the highest-voted AMA-type posts featured:

- Bill Gates

- Elon Musk

- Barack Obama

- A Vacuum Repair Technician

That last one, actually ranked higher in popularity than celebrities Bill Murray and Harrison Ford. It even ranked higher than an AMA with Tim Berners-Lee, the guy who invented the Internet!

This just goes to show that you don't need to have a certain level of notoriety or fame in order to grow your audience with social media. Even a seemingly uninteresting business such as repairing vacuums can prove quite popular when you give others a voice and permission to ask you questions.

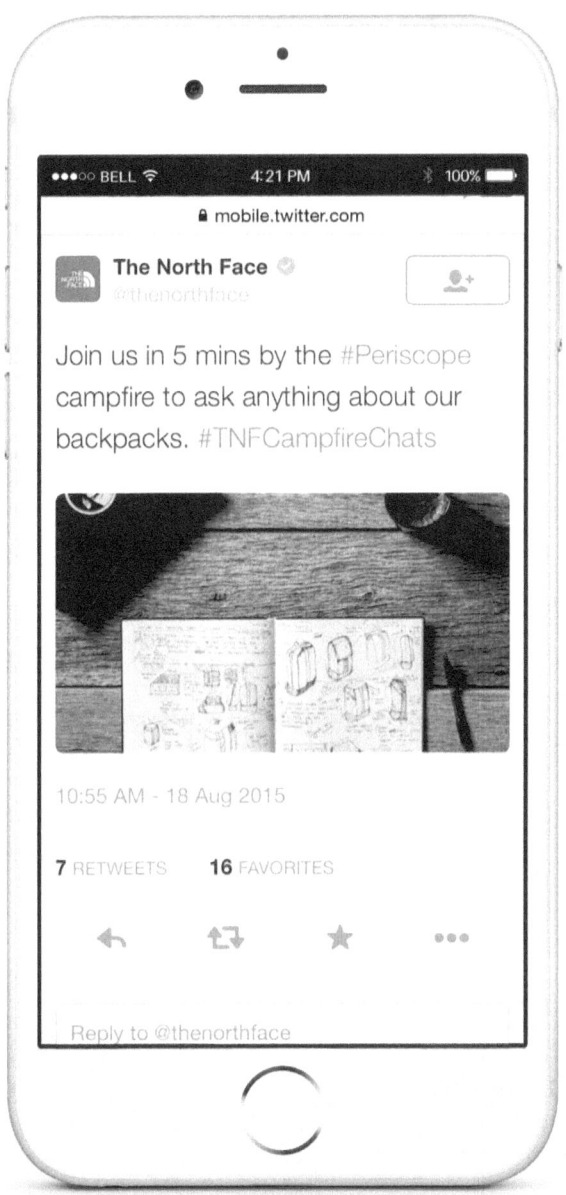

The North Face uses Periscope to answer questions about their

product line

PERSONAL CONNECTION

Sometimes the best business use for a live stream is simply to be yourself. It doesn't always have to be about the business, broadcast something that simply shows a bit of your personality and uniqueness.

I was once sitting on a plane next to a reporter for a major newspaper in Oregon. I asked her about how reporters at her paper are encouraged to use social media to grow their audience. She replied specifically with how they are instructed to use Twitter. She said that they are encouraged to tweet about 80% news content, 20% non-business content. While I'm not sure there is a golden rule for which percentage to attribute to non-professional content, I do believe that there is a strong business case for just connecting with people by being yourself.

PERISCOPE 101: EVERYTHING YOU NEED TO KNOW TO GET STARTED

WHAT IS PERISCOPE?

Periscope is a live-streaming application for both iOS and Android that allows you to stream live video, watch other's videos, participate in comments, give "hearts", and easily share broadcasts as they are happening, or up to 24 hour afterwards.

It was developed by engineers Kayvon Beykpour and Joe Bernstein, and was quickly purchased by Twitter for a reported $100 million in March 2015. On March 26, 2015, Twitter officially re-launched the application on iOS under its own App Store account. Later, on May 26, 2015, Periscope was released for Android.

A live broadcast on Periscope is commonly referred to as a "scope".

WHO CAN VIEW THESE BROADCASTS?

Broadcasts can either be public, available on everyone's global feed (this is the default setting), or private, requiring each viewer to be individually selected. When a broadcast link is shared, either automatically or manually, then people are able to click that link and view the broadcast in their web browser. Technically, people can view your scopes and not even have an account on Periscope. This allows for faster adoption with a lower barrier of entry than other social networks that require a critical mass of users before the tool becomes useful.

WHAT'S UP WITH THE HEARTS?

Think of hearts as a way to add applause to what the broadcaster is saying, or perhaps as a like button that you click over and over again. They not only provide encouraging feedback to the broadcaster, but Periscope keeps account of how many hearts your scope receives, and those with the most hearts over time are featured in the "Most Loved" list.

Hearts are a fun addition to Periscope, and people seem to love them:

"It seems silly, but the multi-heart approach serves a purpose: It lets the people who are recording know that their audience still appreciates what they're doing, even several minutes into a stream. The result is that on popular streams — like that of retired astronaut Chris Hadfield, an early user — hearts fizz furiously in the corner of the screen throughout every broadcast, rising up like soda bubbles."

—The Verge[1]

"But perhaps the greatest part of Periscope — I certainly think it's a highlight — is the fact that you can send hearts to the broadcaster by tapping on the screen. . . . I'll admit I take more than a little joy out of sending lots and lots of hearts to broadcasters whose videos I like perhaps only a little. On the other end as a broadcaster, it feels oddly gratifying to receive these hearts from viewers. I liken it to getting Favorites on Twitter or Likes on Facebook; it taps into that same insecure need for love and recognition (hey, I admit it). It's a very minor feature, but it's one that I find rather delightful."

—Engadget[2]

---

[1]   http://www.theverge.com/2015/3/26/8293353/periscope-live-streaming-twitter-meerkat

[2]   http://www.engadget.com/2015/03/26/periscope/

"In one five-minute broadcast, I got 34 hearts from one person. (I love you too, whoever you are.) A performance from the San Francisco Gay Men's Chorus at Twitter's offices received a constant stream of different-colored hearts on the bottom-right side of the screen throughout the whole performance. It's a clever way to approximate cheering someone on, saying "you're doing great!" while they perform."
— Wired[3]

So, give hearts freely when you want to encourage the broadcaster. There seems to be a 500 heart-count limit per viewer per broadcast. Hearts that are given during a replay do not count towards the heart count total.

WHAT ARE MY OPTIONS WHEN STARTING A BROADCAST?

Once you have created an account, open the Broadcast Tab by clicking on the Camera icon at the bottom of the screen. You can then enter a title that describes your broadcast, and select from a few more icon-driven options:

- **Location**: Whether or not you want to broadcast your coordinates. Probably not a good idea from your home, but encouraged if you are someplace interesting as people can select scopes based off of a world map.

- **Privacy**: Make the broadcast private instead the default public.

---

[3] http://www.wired.com/2015/03/periscope/

- **Chat**: Here you can decide whether you want anyone to be able to comment (the default), or only those people that you follow. This could help deal with trolls (a subject we will dive into later in the book), but also limits the ability to grow your network and increase connections.

- **Twitter**: Because you need a Twitter account to have a Periscope account, you are only a tap away from announcing your scope to the world. Periscope doesn't allow you to schedule a scope, so the link to the broadcast is created as soon as you hit the "Start Broadcast" button. This makes it hard to share the link on Twitter since you will likely be busy getting your broadcast going, so having a tweet go out automatically is quite handy. The format of the Tweet is:

  "LIVE on #Periscope: Your Title http://yourlink.com"

HOW DO PEOPLE DISCOVER BROADCASTS?

There are two main ways someone might enter into the audience of a Periscope broadcast. First of all, they might come in through a link that you shared, or that someone else that they follow shared. While these types of viewers are more likely to stick around because they were led there by someone they trust, they are also more likely to be a "web watcher", since they came in via a link, and will not have the ability to comment or leave hearts.

The second way that someone enters into a broadcast is by browsing the list of what is being broadcast live. This can be pretty entertaining, and certainly can become a time-vacuum (much like entering into a YouTube binge). In one sitting you can view and converse with someone feeding monkeys in Brasil, enjoy a backstage view of a concert in New York, and see what a skydiver sees as they approach the ground in New Zealand.

If someone that you follow posts a broadcast within the last 24 hours, you will see their scope listed under "Recent Broadcasts". The Periscope team also hand-selects a few "Featured" scopes to list here as well, based off of their quality and how interesting they are.

HOW DO I FIND AND FOLLOW PEOPLE ON PERISCOPE?

When you first sign up for Periscope, you are given the option to follow others whom you already follow on Twitter. As mentioned previously, there is also a "Most Loved" list in the people tab within the app, but I find this to be of limited use since some activities that generate a lot of hearts are not necessarily from accounts that I want to be following.

A more reliable way to build up a list of people to follow is simply browse the live scopes, and follow people who are doing interesting things. You can also click on the commenters within a broadcast and follow them if they seem to be adding value to the conversation. After one of your own broadcasts, watch the replay and follow some of your top commenters.

Realize that these are the same methods that people are going to be using to find you on Periscope, so this is another reason to be helpful and leave thoughtful comments on other people's scopes.

HOW DO NOTIFICATIONS WORK WITH PERISCOPE?

Like any mobile app, notifications can be turned on or off. Periscope is no exception, with a few more granular controls to limit what notifications you receive. If you want to take in all of the Periscope notifications life has to offer, you will see notifications for the following events:

- Someone starts following you: "Ryan Battles (@ryanbattles) started following you."

- Someone you follow starts a public broadcast: "Ryan Battles is live: 10 Marketing Tips for Entrepreneurs."

- Someone you follow invites you to a private broadcast: "Ryan Battles invited you to a private broadcast: Discussing new ideas, your input requested."

- Somebody you follow shares another person's live broadcast. "@ryanbattles wants you to watch: Pat Flynn is live: Behind the Scenes of SPI"

- When someone you follow on Twitter live broadcasts for the first time

WHAT IF THE CHAT GETS DISTRACTING?

Live interaction can be a wonderful thing, but it can also become a big distraction to either the viewer trying to see more of the screen, or a broadcaster trying to complete a thought. Perhaps you want to save questions and answers to the end, and don't want to see comments flying by as you record your broadcast.

Thankfully, Periscope allows you to turn off chat by swiping right in iOS or swiping up in Android and tapping "Hide Chat". The same can be done on a web viewer by pressing "h" during the stream, although by simply stretching your browser window to be wider than it is tall, you move the comments off to the side of the window.

Even though comments are hidden from you, they are still visible and able to be entered by the audience, you can also see these comments during the replay.

IS THERE A LIMIT TO THE COMMENTING?

Comments can quickly spiral out of control when you have 1,000 viewers tuning in at the same time. Periscope has a built-in mechanism to turn off chat for users over a certain limit (although they can still view the comments, they cannot leave any comments themselves). This limit is not hard-set, but is instead based upon the network conditions of the broadcaster and viewers, as well as how early people join the broadcast.

CAN I BLOCK A COMMENTER?

Yes, this is the Internet and there will be hecklers. If you find that you need to block a user, you can click on their name (next to their comment), and click "Block User". You can unblock people at any time.

When someone is blocked, they are no longer able to:

- Follow you

- View any of your broadcasts

- Leave comments

- Give hearts

Remember that blocking is much more than simply muting them, so be sure to use it accordingly. I'd hate to "block" someone for asking too many questions when in reality I just wish they were "muted" but could still watch (which unfortunately is not currently possible).

MAKING A FIRST IMPRESSION: OPTIMIZING YOUR BIO

By default, your username, description, and profile photo are set to be your Twitter values when you sign up for Periscope, but you have a chance to change them to something custom before completing registration.

YOUR USERNAME

Like many social media networks, once you set your username in Periscope, you cannot change it without creating a new account.

This makes selecting your username something important to consider from the get-go (if you have already registered, you can use another Twitter account to create a new Periscope account).

Some people swear by using a crafty business name as their title (i.e. @screwthe9tofive), some people prefer to simply use their given names (i.e. @PatFlynn). If you are the official account for an organization, it makes sense to use that organization's name, or perhaps a hybrid approach (i.e. @RyanFromHarpoon).

One thing to remember when choosing a name on Periscope is that this is what people will see when you are commenting on their scopes, so a username that reflects your personal name (assuming it is easy to pronounce) can be an easier way for the broadcaster to call you out personally while scoping.

YOUR DESCRIPTION

Unlike your username, fortunately you can change your bio at any time. Here are a few suggestions to keep in mind when optimizing your description:

- You only have 160 characters, the same as a Twitter bio.

- Think strategically about keywords. Words used in your bio will allow you to come up in search results on Periscope. When people are searching for others to connect with on this new platform, leveraging search terms can be a key strategy.

- No need for hashtags. On Twitter, people search using hashtags, but the same isn't the case with Periscope. While people still name their scopes using hashtags (because of the auto Tweeting of the scope title once it gets started), there isn't much use for hashtags within a description.

- Be professional, yet interesting. Any personal information that you can throw in there that shows your human side is a nice touch, but you still need to mention why someone should follow you from a professional standpoint. Here is a nice sample bio that is both professional and unique: "Sketch Comedy Actor. Pratfalls and impersonations are my specialty. Raised in Montana, I'm the youngest of five kids, and I love hiking, snow boarding, surfing, and fly-fishing with my dad."

- Avoid using the words "Authority", "Expert" and "Guru". These are overused, and like Margaret Thatcher said, "Power is like being a lady; if you have to say you are, you aren't". Instead of describing yourself as an authority on something, instead talk about what makes you that authority and let the audience draw their own conclusions.

- Use a full link URL. Instead of saying "Check out ryanbattles.com for more info", the statement would be better written "Check out https://ryanbattles.com for more info." This is because when someone is viewing your profile in a web interface, a full URL is clickable (while in the mobile app neither form is clickable).

- If you are related to another handle on Twitter, use that as @username. For example, in my bio I have "Co-founder of @HarpoonApp". While this isn't clickable, it is understood to be a Twitter handle and people will know how to use that to find out more information. It is a succinct way to connect people to some other accounts that you might want to direct them to.

YOUR PROFILE PHOTO

It's nice that Periscope automatically ports over your Twitter photo, and in most cases, this is the recommended avatar to use. By using the same photo for various social accounts, you begin to establish a brand identity.

On a crisp fall afternoon a couple years ago I was in an outdoor photo shoot with my family, wearing a newsboy-style cap. Towards the end of this session I asked the photographer to take a few head-shots that I might use for my online profiles. One of the photos stood out to me, and I currently use it on just about every account I own.

Earlier this year I attended a conference in Las Vegas for entrepreneurs, and knew that some people who I converse with on Twitter will be there, and this will be the first time we meet in person.
Knowing that they have only seen me with that cap on for the most
part, I decided that I would wear that every day of the conference.
As expected, a handful of people commented that they recognized
me immediately thanks to the hat. The point is, using consistency
across platforms will help build a brand identity that you can leverage even in face-to-face meetings.

GO IN WITH A PLAN: THE ANATOMY OF AN EFFECTIVE SCOPE

Alright, you've set up your profile, you've learned what Periscope is all about and have perhaps even viewed a few scopes from other people. It's time to start your own broadcasts.

Of course, you could just wing it and start your scope without much planning. That's perfectly acceptable in the Periscope world, and is honestly what most people do anyway.

However, I've noticed by observing a great deal of scopes that some tactics are practiced consistently by people who are winning with Periscope for their business. There are key points to touch upon during your scope that will maximize sharing, following, and helpful feedback.

SCHEDULE YOUR BROADCASTS

With Periscope, you can't technically schedule your scope within the app, but that doesn't mean that you can't promote the scope on your other networks beforehand.

If you use a social media scheduling tool like Buffer[1] or Hootsuite[2], you can fill out a sequence of reminder messages to go out automatically across your social networks in the hours and minutes leading up to your broadcast. For an added bonus, you can create a graphic to share explaining what you will be exploring during your scope. You can create this graphic using the free online graphics tool Canva.[3]

Of course, when you schedule your broadcasts you need to ensure that they start on time, and that when you announce them you provide your time zone since your followers may be anywhere else in the world.

PUT YOUR PHONE ON AIRPLANE MODE

This tip is commonly forgotten, but the last thing you want to have happen is to receive a phone call or text message in the middle

---

[1]   https://buffer.com
[2]   https://hootsuite.com/
[3]   https://www.canva.com/

of your scope. An easy way to silence all notifications is to put your phone in Airplane mode.

This assumes that you have wi-fi for your connection, instead of the cell signal. If you are broadcasting from a remote location, this might not be a possibility. Another choice would be to put your phone into "Do Not Disturb" mode.

To turn on Do Not Disturb mode on an iPhone, swipe up from the bottom of the screen to open Control Center, then tap the crescent moon.

For Android, you can silence notifications via the volume buttons. Start moving the volume up or down (when there's no music playing) and then tap "None" on the pop-up dialog that appears.

DO A QUICK CAMERA CHECK

Don't wait until your scope starts to check your camera angle. You can simply turn on your phone's camera to set up the right position, or wait to start your scope until after you've ensured that you have everything set within the preview window.

It is generally more flattering to have the camera at or slightly above eye-level. Way too many people are scoping with phones sitting on their desk, and the world gets to have a front-row seat to a look up their nostrils.

CRAFT A KILLER TITLE

Whether you are writing a blog post, a book, an email subject, or a Periscope title, you need to write something that grabs attention. If people never click on your scope because the title is unappealing, it doesn't matter how awesome your broadcast is inside.

To write an effective title, try to focus on one of these strategies:

- Use numbers. People are drawn to number-driven headlines for a variety of reasons. Whether it makes them question how many of them they already knew, or if they like the finite number of tips they will receive, number-driven titles like "The 5 Things You Need to Know About X" are sure to get some curious clicks.

- Use interesting adjectives. These of course can be overused and lose their effectiveness, but turning "A Guide to Growing Tomatoes" into "The Simple Guide to Growing Tomatoes with Minimal Effort" can mean the difference between a well-attended broadcast and one with just a few viewers.

- Get Specific. A general title like "Write a Song" generates very little interest, but turn that into "How to Compose Your Own Song: Songwriting 101" and a lot more intrigue is sure to be created.

- Foster Distrust. Nobody likes to feel like they are being taken advantage of, so tapping into that with a headline like

"Is Your Doctor Telling You the Truth About Vaccines?" is an emotional hack that draws in viewers.

- Ask Questions. A title that is simply a question encourages people to click into the scope to find out if they are correct. Something like "Do You Know the #1 Cause of Most Automobile Crashes?" is much more attractive than "Distracted Driving Lecture."

- Use Scarcity. If people feel as if they have brief chance to partake in something (which is technically the case with all Periscope broadcasts), then call it out in your headline. Turn "See behind the scenes" to "Quick! For the next 10 minutes, let us take you behind the scenes."

- Call Out Exclusivity. We all love to be a part of something exclusive, so try a title additives like "See behind closed doors" or "Get a Periscope-only sneak peak."

The principles that make good headlines work across a variety of mediums, so if you really want to level-up your title creation muscles, read up more on how to create effective email subjects, or creating headlines that get results.

One thing you don't want to be on Periscope is ambiguous about what your subject matter is. There are a lot of people lurking on the site just to leave suggestive comments or to flirt with others. These folks tend to stay away from business-oriented scopes and click on more mysterious ones, like "Say Hi." Stating the professional nature of your scope will keep your audience targeted and avoids some of the riff-raff that is prevalent on the Internet.

USE EMOJI CHARACTERS

Spend about 10 seconds on Periscope and you'll notice an deluge of emoji characters throughout headlines, usernames, and comments. This is because the only way you can enter text into the Periscope system is through your mobile device, and these all come with emoji keyboards.

Like them or not, those who use them stand out. You don't have to go overboard in order to make an impact, sometimes just using one or two in your title is enough to make it stand out against the text-only titles. Since the text is in black, the emoji characters add a touch of color as people are scrolling through titles on Periscope.

When leaving comments on others' scopes, a well placed emoji can also ensure that the broadcaster sees your comment if a stream is going by.

CONSIDER YOUR SCOPE'S THUMBNAIL

The first thing that the camera sees when starting your broadcast becomes a blurred-out thumbnail for others to see while browsing Periscope. Instead of starting the broadcast pointing at your shoes before lifting the camera up, point the camera at something interesting before turning back to the main subject.

I'm starting to see some marketers create a simple slide on their computer with the camera pointed at it to start the broadcast. Again, because the thumbnails are blurred I wouldn't worry too hard about more than simply a large, bold title and perhaps a simple graphic. You can also take advantage of a bold background color in your slide in order to pop in a sea of typically dull or dark scope thumbnails.

TICK THE TWITTER BIRD TO AUTO-TWEET YOUR START

We covered this briefly in a previous chapter, but it needs to be re-iterated. Unless this is a private broadcast, you're going to want to have a link to the scope tweeted out immediately when you start. Some of your followers will see this link go live and might jump in as web viewers. At the very least, they can catch your 24-hour replay.

UNTICK THE LOCATION BROADCAST IF YOU ARE AT HOME

Geolocation can sometimes be a little off, but sometimes it can be very precise. Unless you want the world to know your home address, make sure to untick the location broadcast icon before starting.

GREET THE REPLAY VIEWERS

When you first start broadcasting your scope, you will be the only one in the room. However, when your scope is clicked on for the 24-hour replay, all of your replay viewers start from the beginning. Because of this, make the first words out of your mouth directed towards replay viewers.

Say "hi" to the replay viewers, and remind them that they can still leave hearts during a replay, encouraging them to do so. You can also remind them to subscribe to your feed so that they are notified next time you go live.

After you start to see a handful of live viewers pour in, then your language can adjust to include the live audience.

GREET PEOPLE BY NAME

The biggest differentiator for Periscope vs. a YouTube video is that the viewers can interact with you in real time. People love to hear their name spoken out loud by the person they are watching, so spend a few seconds saying hi individually to those who are joining your scope.

You can also ask people where they are from, which is not only useful for you as the broadcaster, but entertaining for the rest of the viewers to realize that they are part of a global chat. It also provides some filler content while people are joining the room before you dive in to your subject at hand.

CALL OUT FIRST TIMERS

If someone has seen 5 of your broadcasts, odds are that they're a fan and will see more in the future. For many people, however, this might be their first time tuning into your content. Make these people feel special by letting them know you want to know who they are. Asking the first-time viewers to type in "First" to the chat window while you welcome them by name brings them one step closer to becoming a follower of yours, and enhances that personal connection.

ASK FOR HEARTS

This one feels silly at first to most people, but the truth is, the hearts matter on Periscope and they help others to find your broadcast by bringing it higher in the rankings. Your hearts also stick with your username, so adding them to your account brings a sense of credibility when people are viewing your profile.

You can say something as simple as "I also want to remind you to leave hearts by tapping on the screen if there is something that you especially agree with or enjoyed. This helps me to know what works for my audience." If you watch the replay of the scope, let the viewers know that you go back through and take note of when the hearts are shared so you know how to create better content. There are ways that you can ask for hearts that put the viewers best interests first, vs simply asking for hearts because you want to rise in the ranks.

ASK FOR SHARES

In an ideal world, people will spontaneously share content that they enjoy. In some cases, this is true. However, in most cases, a gentle nudge to share is all that is needed to make a big difference in how far an idea is spread.

A lot of the Periscope Pros know that starting off their broadcast with a call to sharing will increase the audience of that scope. Simply say something like "I want to call attention to the share tools on Periscope, simply click the person icon at the bottom of the screen to tweet out or invite your followers to check this out. Thanks!"

This can also be employed at the end of a broadcast, reminding them to share with folks who would enjoy the replay. For example: "Thanks again for hanging out for the past 10 minutes, if you enjoyed it or found value, please share the link so your friends can enjoy the replay over the next 24 hours." Because you can do a Twitter search for the broadcast link after 24 hours, you could even pair this request with a small reward, like choosing a random viewer who tweets out a link and reaching out to them for a small prize. Because they have to be following you on Twitter in order to receive a direct message from you, this also requires that they follow you on Twitter in order to win. More shares plus followers, definitely worth considering as a strategy.

RELAX

Periscope broadcasts are supposed to be raw and honest. Don't be afraid of stumbling over your words, losing your train of thought, or using excessive "ums". Just talk like you naturally would (this gets easier with practice), and don't script out what you are going to say beforehand word-for-word.

It is smart to have a few bullet points of topics that you might want to cover, or perhaps memorize your introduction statement, but the bulk of your scope should be unscripted and natural. You know how it feels to speak with a customer service agent over the phone that is obviously reading from a script. Phone calls are supposed to sound natural, and so are Periscope broadcasts.

TIE IN OTHER SOCIAL NETWORKS

While people can give you feedback during the broadcast via chat and hearts, you can ask them what they thought about the scope towards the end by pointing them towards your Twitter and Facebook accounts (or whatever your main networks are). I typically hear people saying something like: "We're wrapping up here but I'd really like to know what you thought about this broadcast.

Reach out to me on Twitter at @ryanbattles, or on Facebook by going to ryanbattles.com/facebook. I can't wait to hear from you!"

As an added bonus, you can have a piece of paper or slideshow screen with your Twitter handle and Facebook address showing, and focus your camera on those during this time. Ask them to take a screenshot to follow up after the scope. This is a great way to increase engagement after the broadcast and multiply your efforts.

THANK EVERYONE

Of course, the polite way to end any broadcast is to thank those who have listened in. You can start with a general thank you, and perhaps mention a few of the most active commenters by name. Typically at this time people will be typing in their own goodbye or thank you message, and you can call those people out by name as well. This again just ties in the fact that the broadcast was live and interactive, as opposed to a pre-recorded video.

DEALING WITH TROLLS AND OTHER DISTRACTIONS

On any platform where comments are allowed, the Internet trolls will find a way to be heard. All you need to do is view the comment thread for just about any YouTube video to see how prevalent obnoxious or offensive commenters are.

One of the reasons for trolling on the Internet is perceived anonymity. If you can't see who I am when I type this, why not go a little overboard and say what I would never say to someone in person?

Thankfully, because Periscope accounts are tied to Twitter accounts, there is a tendency to be a little more careful with how you interact with people on Periscope. Of course, it is easy to create a new Twitter account, or perhaps the trolls don't care about their online reputation. Either way, you are likely to deal with them at one time or another.

So what do you do when a commenter is polluting your feed with unhelpful garbage, or offensive talk?

1. Ignore them. Because they are likely trying to get a rise out of you, or see your reaction to what they are saying, sometimes the best defense is to simply ignore them and move on. They will eventually lose interest or get bored with their little game and will take their antics elsewhere. You may also have a handful of people in your audience that will address it for you, telling them to chill out or leave the chat. While this does draw attention to the commenter, it at least doesn't draw your attention to it. Hopefully it will be short-lived, but if someone is continuing to be offensive, then you might want to move on to the next reaction.

2. Block them. You can block a commenter in your stream by clicking in their profile and tapping the block option. This will remove their comments from your scope, they will be kicked out of it, and your future streams will essentially be invisible to them. This is somewhat of a nuclear option, so you don't want to go blocking everyone that says something mildly offensive. Or perhaps you do, just know what it means to block them.

3. Build up your fanbase. Because only the first hundred or so (this varies) viewers can comment, when a room begins to fill up there isn't much room for new people to join in and detract from the conversation. If you have a scheduled scope and invite people in from your social networks, you might fill up the available chat slots with people who already know and support you, so the casual troll perusing Periscope won't have an opportunity to chime in.

NO HEARTS

There is a certain thrill that comes from a volcano of hearts rising as you share your witty and entertaining thoughts with the world. However, there may just be times when you think that you've just dropped a great bit of wisdom into the scope and nobody responds. Perhaps you are going on and on and wondering why nobody is leaving any hearts, don't they like what you are saying?

My advice is to simply ignore the lack of hearts instead of thinking too much about it. For starters, a great deal of the people who will get value out of what you are sharing might be replay viewers, and you don't see their hearts when you are broadcasting live. Another consideration is that the web viewers who are in there because they clicked a link that you shared cannot send hearts either. They are simply passive observers.

After your scope, if you chose to review it, you can then think more critically about the hearts that were left during some moments of the broadcast. If there is measurably more hearts given during some parts of the talk than others, then perhaps that is a takeaway in what is more popular with your audience. During your presentation is not the time to have this reflection as it will likely distract you from moving forward in confidence.

DROPOUTS

When broadcasting a scope, it is fun to see the attendee number begin to rise. For a number of reasons people are tuning in to hear what you have to share. Perhaps they like the title or thumbnail of your scope. Perhaps they are followers of yours on Periscope or Twitter, and jumped in when they heard you were going live. Whatever the reason, it is nice to see a growing attendee list.

When this number of attendees start to drop, the natural inclination is to think that what you are doing is uninteresting to them. However, this is often not the case. The nature of Periscope is that people jump in and out of scopes very quickly because they just want to peek in and see what the person is talking about. They may only have a quick minute or two and just want to see what is going on, but soon have to drop off because of something that has nothing to do with your content.

Again, the advice here is to ignore the rise and fall of attendees and stay the course of your scope. If you have any doubt about this simply watch another person's scope and take note of the ebb and flow of viewers.

DON'T STOP NOW: WHAT TO DO IMMEDIATELY AFTER A SCOPE

After you stop broadcasting your scope, the work is over, right?

Wrong. There's actually quite a bit that you can still do after your scope to maximize its potential. Just because you are no longer live doesn't mean that people can't still benefit from what you shared during the broadcast.

Share the Replay

When your broadcast is over, you can still use the sharing links to encourage those who missed the broadcast to view the replay for the next 24 hours.

If you closed out of the broadcast inside of the app, you can still find the link to the broadcast by either:

1. View your last tweet if you sent one out when the broadcast began. That same link will now direct visitors to the replay window when clicked.

2. In Periscope, click on the television icon at the bottom of the screen to view recent scopes from those you follow. Your broadcasts are also in this mix and you can click on one to find the sharing tools for that particular broadcast.

KATCH.ME

Of course, the 24 hour limit on replays can be a little off-putting to some. Thankfully, there is a service out there that can automatically save all of your scopes and keep them archived for view for an indefinite amount of time. This service can be found at Katch.me.

There are a few caveats with Katch.me, however. First of all, the most obvious is that people can not leave hearts for a replay on Katch, so if you are still within your 24-hour sharing window on Periscope, this might be a better place to send them.

Another negative about a Katch replay is that the comments are not included in the video stream, but they are output as a long strand of text next to the replay window. This makes it difficult to match up a comment that was written to a particular part of the video.

Katch.me is great because you can set it up once by connecting your Periscope account, and have it automatically record every scope moving forward. You can even set it up to automatically tweet out a Katch link to the replay after your scope is over. However, as mentioned previously, the better link to share immediately after your scope is more likely to be the direct Periscope link.

An auto-tweet from Katch after a broadcast from
The Weather Channel

SCREENCASTING

You can overcome the limitations of Katch.me with a little creativity by capturing a screen recording of your scope, and publishing that on YouTube or Vimeo for sharing with your audience. The benefits of this approach is that you capture the hearts and comments along with your video and audio, all in one screen. They are all synced up, so it is essentially the same experience of a native Periscope replay, but without the time limit.

As an added bonus, you may begin to pick up YouTube subscribers if they like your replay and they will begin to receive email notifications when you upload a new broadcast recording.

In order to capture a screen recording, you simply need to copy that replay link from your broadcast, and load it up on your computer. As there is no Periscope app for computers, you will simply watch the replay in a web browser window. What is great about this experience is that if you expand your window to be wider than the narrow screen of a phone, then your comments move off to the left of your video, so they can still be viewed without obscuring what you are sharing.

While watching this replay broadcast, you can use screen recording software like CamStudio for Windows, or QuickTime for Mac. There are fancier screen recording software packages out there, but you don't really need any of those fancy add-ons in order to create a simple replay broadcast. These free tools will suit your needs just fine.

After creating your screen recording, simply upload the video to your service of choice and share away!

Comic artist Todd Nuack records his broadcasts to share
on YouTube

CRITICAL SELF-REVIEW

As a podcaster, one of my favorite podcasts to listen to is my own. Not because I enjoy hearing myself speak, or that I have amnesia and need to remind myself of the tips that I share. The reason why I love listening to my own podcast is that I can hear moments in the podcast when I seemed confident and was on a roll, as well as moments where I sounded unsure and had awkward fillers like "ummm", "like", and "you know". Each time I listen to my own broadcasts I get a tiny bit better at crafting my next one.

The same holds true for Periscope broadcasts. Going back and watching your broadcast will help you to see yourself the way your audience sees you, and what seems to be working or what needs improving. The added benefit of watching a Periscope replay is that you can view comments and hearts given during your scope. Podcasters never get this sort of feedback!

Another nice thing about replaying your own broadcasts is that you can follow others who seem to be leaving interesting comments. Since their Periscope handle is likely their Twitter handle, you can reach out to them on Twitter to thank them for the great conversation, solidifying the connection even more.

A scope only lasts about 5-15 minutes, but the work you put into it both before and afterwards can multiply your reach many times over, and are well worth considering when using Periscope for business.

OPTIONAL EQUIPMENT: SMALL PURCHASES THAT MAKE A BIG IMPACT

While you need nothing more than a mobile device in order to record a Periscope broadcast, there are a few pieces of equipment that can enhance your viewer's experience, and take your scopes to the next level.

Note: for this section I will not be recommending specific products to buy as the market is likely to change as Periscope grows in popularity, and new equipment is launched. To download an updated list, visit https://ryanbattles.com/periscope-bonus

SELFIE STICK

Personally, I think these are funny devices to watch people walking around with, but you can't argue with the genius behind them. Not only are they useful for your vacation shots when there is nobody around to take a photo for you, but they also come in very handy for scoping.

Holding the phone up and away from you while recording provides a more flattering angle to your face, and shows more of your surroundings. It is a purchase worth considering if you find that your camera angle needs improvement or if you are often filming up too close.

Stabilizer

For those who scope on the go—perhaps a real estate agent giving a home tour, or a travel agent showing off an exotic location—shaky cameras can be a hindrance when putting together a video that doesn't give viewers motion sickness.

Fortunately, there are a slew of image stabilizing products out there to help you keep the camera steady while moving. The most basic of stabilizers are simply clamp on handles, that give a more natural grip to the phone to reduce shakiness. Moving up the chain in terms of cost you can find some with strategic weights or even gyroscopes to keep recordings from becoming too jerky.

To stay within a budget, you might want to just go with a selfie stick that will provide the benefits listed above, while providing a more natural grip for carrying your phone during a recording.

TRIPOD

If your Periscope broadcast is going to be from a static location, perhaps outside an area with a nice backdrop, or at your desk where you can share images on your screen, a tripod can help with preventing unnecessary camera vibrations.

There are both floor-resting tripods and desktop models available. The problem with a desktop tripod is that you are likely to be broadcasting up your nostrils from that angle, unless you put the camera up on a shelf higher than your eyes.

A floor-resting tripod can be nice, as long as you have the space to accommodate it. The nice thing about tripods is that they can be relatively inexpensive, with the cheapest being around $20. You will likely also need to purchase a phone tripod mount to hold your phone to the tripod, but these can be purchased for less than $10 on Amazon.

LENSES

The quality of the lens of today's smartphones is utterly amazing. With each upgrade from Apple, Samsung, and others — the photos and videos become better and better.

Why would you ever want to buy an additional lens for a phone?

I'm not talking about purchasing a lens to take a higher quality photo, but instead to add some additional effects to the video being shot.

The biggest improvement that a clip-on lens can provide is a fisheye effect. This effect essentially captures more of the room and compresses it down to the traditional view of the camera. This makes the subject in the center a little larger while making the objects on the periphery a little smaller, the net result can be an attractive way to capture a talking broadcaster and showing more of the room instead of focusing in on just their face.

In addition to fish-eye lenses, there are also wide-angle lenses, which work in a similar way, but only on the horizontal plane instead of a sphere. Another possible enhancement is a macro lens, which makes close-up recordings more clear and detailed.

Can't decide which lens to try out? Fortunately, some companies make all-in-one lens kits so you can swap between these various enhancements. You might find yourself wanting a fisheye while talking to your audience, then switching to a macro lens to show them something in more detail.

LIGHTING

Lighting is one of the most often ignored aspects of amateur video recording, typically settling on using just the overhead lighting of whatever room that they are in.

At the very least, your recordings will look a lot better if you are next to a window, with natural light to enhance the colors that the camera will pick up.

To take things up a notch, you can use a lighting kit to reduce shadows and illuminate you or the subject from a couple of angles. There are some wonderful tutorial videos on how to do lighting for your recordings on wistia.com/blog.

One of the most flattering lights to use when recording yourself is a ring light. This is essentially a circle of light with an absent center that you can use to place the camera. This can be a more complex or expensive setup to attain, but you are almost guaranteed a flattering shot because of it. The exception to this is if you wear glasses. A ring light will cast the most heinous reflection in your glasses and detract from any positives that the lighting brings to the rest of your face.

For quick lighting enhancement using what you already have lying around the house, just add a few lamps or task lights to light up your face better for the camera, hitting a couple of angles to reduce shadowing, and one more to hit the wall behind you so there isn't a shadow.

MICROPHONES

If you are recording in a quiet room, your phone's microphone is going to work great. If you are in a noisier environment, or are standing away from your phone during the recording, you might benefit from an external microphone.

One of the simplest solutions is to purchase a lavalier (clip on lapel) microphone that plugs into your phone's headphone/microphone jack and captures audio closer to your mouth. This also has the benefit of providing consistent audio levels, in cases where you turn your head while speaking or move close to or away from the phone's microphone.

As I mentioned, however, all of this equipment is optional. You don't have to have a closet full of equipment to create high-quality scopes. These tools might just help you overcome a few negatives that your recordings are suffering from due to your unique situation, or just help you set yourself apart from other broadcasters who are producing poor quality videos.

WINNING WITH VIEWING: HOW TO BE AN ACTIVE PARTICIPANT IN OTHERS' SCOPES

Periscope isn't only about the broadcasting, it is a great way to interact with people as a participant as well. Remember all of those tips that I shared previously about calling out your commenters by name, even following them if they were adding value to the conversation? Well, here's your chance to let others do the same for you.

So how do you leverage your position as an audience member to help out the broadcaster?

Give them some positive feedback during the broadcast

It can be a little nerve wrecking for anybody to place themselves in front of a camera for the world to see. If they are just getting started with Periscope, they may be unsure of themselves, and if they have a low following, there is likely to be few people in their scope.

To ease their nervousness, make sure that you type out some positive compliments that will set them at ease. Let them know that there are friendly folks tuning in, and help them to be their best.

TYPE IN URLS OR HELPFUL INFORMATION

When the broadcaster mentions a URL or resource, do them a favor and type it in as a comment so anyone who didn't catch it correctly can have a reference, write it down, or take a screenshot for later. The speaker isn't able to type into the chat window, and there are no "show notes" like there might be with a YouTube video or podcast. I've seen this done by audience members a number of times and it always elicits a "thank you" from the presenter.

ASK QUESTIONS

A lot of comments during a scope can be short little blurbs that don't really spur on any direction for conversation. By thinking about good questions and asking them of the broadcaster, you show them that people are interested in hearing what they have to say, and help to fill up the time with quality information that others might be wondering about as well.

GIVE HEARTS

Another form of encouragement, sending out those little hearts only cost you a tap of the finger on your screen, but provide positive feedback for the presenter. Each time you join a new scope, you have 500 hearts to give away for that broadcast. This number is replenished with each broadcast, so don't worry about ever running out.

USE EMOJI CHARACTERS TO STAND OUT

Like the name you use on Periscope and the titles you give your scopes, using emoji characters on your mobile keyboard will help your comments stand out from the others that are streaming by. Usually only 1 or 2 emoji characters are needed to increase the visibility without coming across as obnoxious.

THANK THEM

At the end of a broadcast, instead of dropping off like most of the viewers will do, take a moment to leave a thoughtful thank you for the presenter. As long as the broadcast is running, the host is able to see your comment. You can also type out your thank you message as you think the broadcaster is wrapping up, waiting to hit send until they officially call it to close.

Above all, when observing a Periscope broadcast, just be a good citizen of the platform and try to do unto others as you would have them do unto you. Following the golden rule is a sure path to fostering positive relationships on any social platform, and will come back around to benefit you in the long run.

ACCELERATION TACTICS: GROWING YOUR PERISCOPE FOLLOWING

When you first join Periscope, you will have 0 followers. How fast this number grows will depend on a few things, and fortunately there are tactics to consider when trying to grow your Periscope audience.

Growing a following on Periscope is important because your followers will receive notifications (unless they turn them off) whenever you start a new broadcast. They will also see your previous broadcasts in the last 24 hours in their list of recent broadcasts upon loading up the app.

Even though the following will help you grow your following a little faster, there really is no substitute for consistently outputting high-quality content to make people want to follow you.

CREATE AN ACCOUNT NOW

Being tied to Twitter, new accounts are encouraged to follow everyone that they already follow on Twitter on the Periscope platform. If they follow you but you don't have a Periscope account yet, you won't be suggested as someone that they follow.

To ensure that the greatest amount of your Twitter followers also follow you on Periscope, create an account as soon as possible so you show up in this recommended listing.

OPTIMIZE YOUR BIO WITH KEYWORDS

Another method people will find your profile is by searching for keywords within the people tab in the app. Personally, I was curious who else was on the platform under the keywords "Entrepreneur", "SaaS", and "ExpressionEngine" (those last two are keywords within the web development industry that I am a part of). I was immediately able to identify some key people that I would like to follow and added them to my list. Now I am notified whenever they publish something.

SCOPE OFTEN

The more you broadcast, the more chances people will have to discover you and follow you. A large amount of Periscope traffic is just people browsing around to see what others are posting, and your title just might catch their eye. Some recommend scoping at least once a day if you are going to be aggressive about building a following.

PARTICIPATE OFTEN

As mentioned in the previous chapter, participating in a broadcast with useful questions and helpful comments might lead to the broadcaster following you after the broadcast. I personally have followed other commenters in a thread that I was observing as well just because they shared high-quality information.

ASK FOR FOLLOWS

When broadcasting, don't be afraid to state to your viewers that they can get notified of your next broadcast by clicking the subscribe button. You should mention this both at the beginning and end of your scope for maximum effect.

Another tactic is to share when you have an upcoming scope on Twitter, and within that tweet mention "Follow me on Periscope to get notified when I go live". Many people in your audience might not know what that is just yet, but the growth of Periscope has been very rapid, and will soon hit it's tipping point where it becomes as commonplace as many of the other social networks we all are familiar with.

RUN A CONTEST

Running a contest can be a very effective way to build up new followers. For example, you could have a running giveaway each week where you give out a free copy of a book, a piece of swag, etc. to a random follower. While you can't easily see who has followed you in the past week specifically, you can state that your contest will be for one lucky follower and encourage them to follow you now to be eligible for this week's giveaway, as well as all future giveaways.

Your mileage will vary with the giveaway tactic, but it is certainly worth trying to test the response rate and subscriber growth.

SHARE ON OTHER NETWORKS

By sharing your scopes on your other social networks, you can pull from your most valuable resource: people who are already following you somewhere else.

You can get creative with how you reach out to them. While people are still learning what Periscope actually is, you can be the one to introduce them to it by sharing a link to a screencast of your scope on YouTube, and let them know that if they want to be a part of the conversation to download the app and follow you.

Again, don't be afraid to ask for follows, post high-quality content frequently, and be a good citizen of Periscope, and your following will grow naturally and steadily.

TAKING IT FURTHER: CONVERTING PERISCOPE VIEWERS INTO CUSTOMERS

In a book about using Periscope for business, I would be remiss if I didn't mention how to actually convert your viewers into customers! Perhaps you are running a non-profit and are looking to raise awareness, perhaps you are selling online courses, or even just trying to increase brand awareness, you should have some sort of conversion goal for your viewers on Periscope.

If you try to sell something directly on your scope, you will run the risk of coming across like a simple infomercial, and who would want to follow that type of account unless you have unusually attractive and useful merchandise that sells itself.

LEAD MAGNETS

Instead of selling your product or "big ask" directly to your audience on Periscope, a better tactic is to use a lead magnet that is free, and only requires an email address in order to receive it. For example, you can use LeadPages[1] to create a landing page that describes what your lead magnet is, and requires that they enter their email address in order to receive it.

Examples of items that can be used as lead magnets:

- A video course that can be accessed all at once

- A video course that is spread out over a period of days

- A useful infographic

- A calendar (i.e. Gardening Calendar)

- A recommendation list (i.e. Recommended Gear)

- A checklist for completing a desired task

- A "cheat-sheet" that summarizes some key ideas

- A PDF eBook, it doesn't have to be long

- A short consultation

---

[1]   http://www.leadpages.net

- A coupon

- A ticket to an event

- A free sample

- Access to a private Facebook group or other community/membership site.

- An entrance into a giveaway

- Access to a webinar

- Access to an online tool, like an assessment or estimate calculator

All of these ideas (with the exception of consultations) can be set up to run programmatically, without a need for you to do any manual work when someone signs up.

FOLLOWING UP WITH AUTOMATION

After someone hands over their email address in exchange for something free, next you have to work on "warming up" that lead with a handful of emails that continue to provide value and provide them with something for nothing.

You want to be sure to spread these emails out over a few days, but essentially you are following up with them in order to:

- Build trust

- Establish yourself as an authority

- Foster positive feelings towards your brand

- Warm them up for the big ask (the sale)

One item missing from that list is actually asking for the sale, and that is definitely an email that you want to send out, but not before you've sent out at least one or two emails delivering pure value without asking for anything in return.

An example email campaign auto responder might look something like this:

1. Welcome email, thanking them for signing up and introducing yourself and how you can help them.

2. Helpful content

3. Helpful content

4. Promotion and ask for a sale (bonus if you can relate how that would be helpful to them based off of what you shared in the previous two emails).

5. Helpful content

6. Helpful content

7. Promotion and ask for a sale

This sequence can go on for a long time, as long as you can build content to keep the sequence going. Of course, if they are really not interested they will eventually unsubscribe from your auto responders, but that's okay because it is all a part of qualifying leads, and it is nice when your email sequence does the qualifying for you automatically!

You will also want to choose an email marketing tool that allows behavior-based automation, so when a person does make a purchase you can remove those promotion and sale emails and only provide them with the helpful content, or move them out of that sequence into one that promotes a different product.

Does this all sound complex? It can be overwhelming at first, but thankfully there are email and marketing automation tools that can handle all of these complexities for you, with an attractive and easy-to-use interface as well.

My two recommended tools for email marketing automation are:

1. ConvertKit - https://convertkit.com/

2. Drip - https://www.getdrip.com/

They are both built by a solid team of marketers and developers and are solid choices for someone looking to build their email list and customer base through email marketing. Both of those tools also provide integration with a number of services like LeadPages that make your life easier by automating much of your process.

THANK YOU PAGES

Whether you are redirecting people to a thank you page for providing you with their email, or after they have made a purchase, too many people waste this valuable real estate by having a plain thank you page.

Instead of simply saying "Thank you for your purchase", why not spice it up with "Thank you for your purchase, click the links below to follow us on Twitter and Facebook". They may already follow you on these platforms, and if so, there is nothing lost here by asking again. However, if they are not yet following you on these two platforms, then you increase your following by asking right at the time their trust is at a high level. They've just finished providing you with something, they are much more likely to deepen the relationship by following you on a social network.

Now our strategy has come full-circle. If they follow you on Twitter and Facebook, they are likely to see your announcements of new scopes, and will grow your attendance when you scope, foster more comments, and sharing within their own networks. The longer you stay at this, the more the results grow exponentially. If you are successfully converting a portion of your viewers into subscribers and customers, then your business will grow exponentially as well.

CONCLUSION: WHERE IS PERISCOPE HEADING?

In 2006, Twitter launched as a platform for "microblogging", or sharing 140-character thoughts with the world. As a blogger, I thought this was the dumbest idea ever. Why would you want to use a platform that makes it almost impossible to publish a complete thought? My prediction: Twitter was a waste of the early investor's money and would die a quick death.

Spoiler alert: I was wrong about that.

While Twitter started out with the reputation as a silly tool that the kids were using to upload photos of their food with the obligatory "nom nom nom", it is now regarded as a crucial tool for networking, promotion and advertising, with a value of about $30 billion.

In 2010 the iPad was released. I owned an iPhone, I owned a laptop, I had no need for a machine that fell between those two in usage. "Tablets are silly" I would say to myself, and was convinced that there would never be a market for tablets when smart phones were capable of so much.

Spoiler alert: I was wrong about that too.

Between 2013 and 2017, the tablet market is estimated to increase fivefold. In our own household we own three tablets alone (an old iPad 1 for the kids, and my wife and I each own a mini for eBooks and misc. use).

I was a pretty easy sell on Periscope the first time I saw it. It was just like YouTube, but quicker and easier to create a video, and live commenting. What could be better?

At first I tried to explain it to my wife and she was naturally skeptical. Why would someone use this tool? However, a few nights later when my daughters were live-scoping with Idina Menzel, the voice behind Disney's Frozen character Elsa, she came to realize that this tool just created a whole new world of accessibility where there was none before.

I began sharing with her the use cases of various companies mentioned previously in this book, and as we opened up Periscope together we saw a broadcast of a Southwest Airlines employee describing the planning that goes into stocking the beverages and food aboard a 737. It was something we often took for granted, and were now witnessing how it was done. One thing is for sure, I'm going to remember that broadcast every time I drink a soda during a Southwest flight.

Where is Periscope heading? I'm not sure. We're only scratching the surface of creativity with the tool, as it has only been around for a few months as of this book's writing. I look forward to writing another edition of this book as the tool evolves and new excited uses are discovered.

If you haven't already, join up and start broadcasting — become one of the innovators that are exploring new and exciting ways to grow your business with live streaming.

If you discover a use that helps out your business, reach out and let me know! I'd love to promote your story with others.

I can be reached at hello@ryanbattles.com. Thanks for reading!

LET'S STAY CONNECTED

Thanks for reading along. I'd love to hear your thoughts on Periscope, anything you enjoyed about this book, constructive criticism, and general feedback.

While you can feel free to reach out to me directly at the contact info below, something that would help me out tremendously is if you could leave some feedback on Amazon, simply search for "Periscope for Business" where you'll find this book listed, and leave me an honest review. It is much appreciated.

If you'd prefer to reach out to me directly instead of (or in addition to) leaving an Amazon review, here's my contact info:

- **Email**: hello@ryanbattles.com

- **Twitter**: @ryanbattles

- **Periscope**: ryanbattles

- **LinkedIn**: linkedin.com/in/ryanbattles

- **Facebook**: facebook.com/ryanmbattles

I also have a blog and newsletter, where I post articles on entrepreneurship, productivity, and growing your audience. If you download my bonus materials introduced in the beginning of this book, you'll be included in hearing about new posts and future books (and discounts).

To join the list and download the bonus materials, simply head over to:

https://ryanbattles.com/periscope-bonus

Again, thanks for your time and I look forward to connecting!

Sincerely,

Ryan Battles

YOU MAY ALSO ENJOY

This is officially my third book, and depending upon your line of work, you might be interested in my other three works (one of them is free!):

THE 9 HABITS OF SUCCESSFUL ENTREPRENEURS

This book is the result of my own research on habits that I consistently heard other entrepreneurs talking about as key to their success. Some of them I was already practicing, and some of them I started practicing while doing research for the book. As a result, my own business has grown, my productivity has increased, and my stress levels have gone down.

This book is available on Amazon, just search for "Habits of Successful Entrepreneurs" to find the link. It is available in Print and Kindle formats (audiobook coming soon).

THE 5 HABITS THAT DERAIL ENTREPRENEURS

This mini-book is actually a free download! It is the companion to the 9 Habits book, and dives into the bad habits that are commonplace amongst entrepreneurs, and how to avoid them. Download for free at ryanbattles.com/5-habits

SAAS MARKETING ESSENTIALS

When I'm not writing, I also run a few businesses online that make a recurring income. One of these is known as "Software as a Service" (SaaS), where people pay a monthly fee in order to use the web-based app.

This book has set out to be a guide to growing your own software-based business by researching your target audience, nailing their biggest pain points, and turning your customers into evangelists for your product.

If you're interested, this book is available only on my own site, at ryanbattles.com/saas. There are several packages available with bonus video interviews, downloads, and an audio version.

www.ingramcontent.com/pod-product-compliance
Lightning Source LLC
Chambersburg PA
CBHW030702190526
45164CB00004B/252